TRAPEZE, PERCH POLES, AND OTHER HIGH-FLYING CIRCUS SCIENCE

by Marcia Amidon Lusted

Consultant:
Vesal Dini, PhD in Physics
Postdoctoral Scholar at
Tufts University
Center for Engineering Education Outreach
Medford, Massachusetts

CAPSTONE PRESS
a capstone imprint

Edge Books are published by Capstone Press,
1710 Roe Crest Drive, North Mankato, Minnesota 56003
www.mycapstone.com

Library of Congress Cataloging-in-Publication Data
Names: Lusted, Marcia Amidon, author.
Title: Trapeze, perch poles, and other high-flying circus science / by Marcia
  Amidon Lusted.
Description: North Mankato, Minnesota : Capstone Press, a Capstone imprint,
  [2017] | Series: Edge books. Circus science | Includes bibliographical
  references and index. | Audience: 4 to 6.
Identifiers: LCCN 2017012461|
ISBN 9781515772842 (library binding) |
ISBN 9781515772880 (eBook PDF)
Subjects: LCSH: Aerialists—Juvenile literature. | Circus
  performers—Juvenile literature. | Circus—Juvenile literature.
Classification: LCC GV1817 .L87 2017 | DDC 791.3/4—dc23
LC record available at https://lccn.loc.gov/2017012461

Editorial Credits
Abby Colich, editor; Heidi Thompson, designer; Kelly Garvin,
media researcher; Laura Manthe, production specialist

Photo Credits
Alamy: Chuck Franklin, 26, Daniel Romero/VWPics, 25, EPA, 9, Nathan King, 5, RE-
UTERS, cover, Shockpix Select, 20, theatrepix, 23; Getty Images: Fred Lee/Contributor,
13, Joseph Okpako, 6-7, The Sydney Morning Herald, 17; iStockphoto/Massimo Merlini,
11; Newscom: Japaridze Mikhail/ZUMA Press, 29, Rouelle Umali Xinhua News Agency,
14-15; Shutterstock/chaoss, 18

Artistic elements: Shutterstock: 21, benchart, Gun2becontinued, Igor Vitkovskiy, mik-
ser45, Milissa4like, Nimaxs, Roberto Castillo, s_maria, Supphachai Salaeman

Printed In the United States of America.
010364F17

TABLE OF CONTENTS

FLYING HIGH AT THE CIRCUS

Step right up into the big top. Then look up to see some of the world's most amazing circus acts. An acrobat flies through the air from one trapeze to another. Performers leap onto a board and bounce and flip. Another performer climbs a tall pole and balances on the top, while one person holds the pole steady from below. Hear the audience gasp in amazement.

These high-flying acts are some of the most exciting in the circus. Performers swing, flip, and fly through the air wowing audiences. There is one important element to these amazing acts that should not be overlooked. That element is science. With science, we can better understand how these acts work.

DO NOT TRY THIS AT HOME

The circus is fun to watch, but DO NOT try any of these acts yourself. Circus performers spend years training. They practice every day. Performing a circus act without the proper training and correct safety precautions could result in serious injury. Instead, simple activities that you CAN TRY are included in the pages that follow. They will help you understand the science behind the circus. They are safe, easy, and fun!

SWINGING TRAPEZE

Look up! The circus is starting! High above the center ring, a performer stands on a tiny platform. In front of her is a bar between two ropes hanging down from above. With one smooth motion, she grasps this trapeze and swings from her perch. Back and forth she goes — until she suddenly releases the bar. The audience gasps! Immediately, a performer on a second trapeze grabs her hands. She continues to swing from the arms of her fellow trapeze artist.

What is the science behind the swinging trapeze? As the performer swings on the trapeze, her body behaves like a **pendulum**. A pendulum is a weight that swings back and forth from a fixed point. An initial **force** gets a pendulum moving. In this case, that initial force comes when the trapeze artist jumps off the platform, and **gravity** pulls her down. As it pulls her down, the rope that's fastened prevents her from falling all the way, and allows her to move in an arc, back and forth. The performer pumps her legs to keep the trapeze moving. If the artist doesn't continue to exert this force, the air, along with where the trapeze is attached to the ceiling, will provide the **friction** that slows her down until she stops.

pendulum—a body hung from a fixed point that swings freely back and forth
force—an interaction that changes the motion of an object
gravity—an attractive force that exists between any two objects, including between Earth and everything on it
friction—a force that opposes the relative motion of two or more surfaces in contact

DON'T
TRY THIS
AT HOME

TRY THIS
INSTEAD

A regular playground swing uses the same science as a trapeze. It is also a pendulum. Hop on one to experience forces at work. Think about gravity as the swing moves you back and forth. After you push off, how many times can you swing each way before you slow down to a stop?

STATIC
TRAPEZE

The trapeze acts are just getting started. A new aerialist arrives on the stage. She jumps onto a trapeze. The bar rises up into the air on its ropes. This trapeze doesn't swing. The performer doesn't fly off. But her stunts are no less mesmerizing. She does flips around the bar, balances across it, and climbs up the rope with her legs.

How does the performer manage to stay atop the **static** trapeze? It's all about balance. To stay balanced, the performer must pay close attention to her **center of mass**. The center of mass is the average point of mass distribution in a body. In other words, it's a body's balancing point. The performer's balancing point must stay directly above the static trapeze. If she moves this balancing point too far one way or the other, she falls. Performers learn to make tiny adjustments to their positions so that they can balance themselves under seemingly impossible conditions.

CIRCUS FACT

Ariel performer Ann Cochrane set a world record for the highest static trapeze act. In March 2016 she performed while suspended from a hot air balloon, 10,365 feet (3,159 meters) above the coast of New Zealand.

static—having the quality of being at rest
center of mass—the point in an object around which its mass is evenly distributed

MULTIPLE TRAPEZE

The trapeze acts have been great so far. But wait! There's more! The last trapeze bar is replaced with a new one. This one is wider — and longer. There are two bars instead of one. One performer climbs up and jumps onto the top bar. Three more performers climb onto the lower bar. Just like the previous trapeze acts, the performers swing from their knees, flip around the bar, and hang upside down. It's amazing!

How do they do it? As with the static trapeze, the center of mass is important. But in this multiple trapeze, the importance is four-fold. Each performer must know how to keep her center of mass in the right place on the trapeze — and in relation to the other performers. The performers spend months practicing and coordinating their movements so that they do not bump into each other. Their timing must be perfect, or they run the risk of hitting each other during the performance.

IRON JAW

The trapeze is a tough act to follow, but this next one won't let you down. A performer makes his way below a large metal frame. He reaches for something hanging above his head. He puts it in his mouth. He clamps down, using his teeth and jaws to hold on. He gives a signal, and suddenly he is lifted high into the air. He begins to spin around. He's holding on with only his mouth. It makes you cringe, but you can't look away from this iron jaw!

How is it possible for a man to be held up by just his mouth? This act requires sheer jaw strength. It is important for him to not use just his teeth, but his jaw muscles also. The jaw muscles begin behind the teeth. The jaws create a force that holds onto the mouthpiece. The average man can create 150 pounds (68 kilograms) of force with his molars (back teeth) clenching his jaw. Women can make about 108 pounds (49 kg) of force.

CIRCUS FACT

Some iron jaw performers have no teeth of their own. They perform the act with false ones!

CHINESE POLE

These circus acts have you at the edge of your seat! You can't wait for what's next. Two tall poles appear in the center ring. Two performers climb up each. They stretch and bend their bodies in different ways. They even hold themselves out from the pole at a 90-degree angle like a flag waving in the wind. You wonder how they do it!

Several factors come in to play in the Chinese pole. Friction — the resistance of motion between two objects — lets the performers climb the pole without sliding back down. Staying atop the pole and performing the routine requires great body strength, especially as they hold their bodies out like a flag. During this part, we see **static equilibrium**. This means the person is not moving and is in balance. It happens when all the forces acting on the body sum to zero.

CIRCUS FACT

The Chinese pole has been performed for hundreds of years. One variation is the Danish pole. The pole is fastened to a turntable and has a rope on the top. The pole hangs at an angle as the performers do their routine.

static equilibrium—a state of balance between two or more opposing forces

AERIAL HOOP

A large steel hoop, which looks like a giant hula hoop, hangs low over the center ring. A performer climbs onto the ring, bracing her hands and feet against the inside. Slowly, the aerial hoop, attached to ropes, rises high into the air. The performer hangs from her knees. Then she breaks into splits. She flips around the hoop so fast that it begins a quick spinning motion, but she doesn't fall.

How is this possible? The performer relies on her body strength to hold onto the hoop as she performs her routine. To get herself to spin, she creates a **torque**. Torque is a force acting at a distance from an **axis** that gets an object **rotating**. As the hoop and the performer rotate together, they gain **angular momentum**. Angular momentum is the amount of "oomph" an object has as it rotates. Angular momentum changes as a torque acts. In the end, the hoop will keep spinning until an opposing torque acts to slow it down and decrease its angular momentum.

CIRCUS FACT

In July 2016 Erendira Wallenda performed on an aerial hoop suspended from a helicopter. She hung 150 feet (45.7 meters) above the ocean and completed 35 spins.

torque—the tendency of a force to rotate an object about an axis
axis—the straight line around which an object rotates
rotate—to turn in a circle
angular momentum—a measure of an object's rotation, involving mass,
    shape, and speed

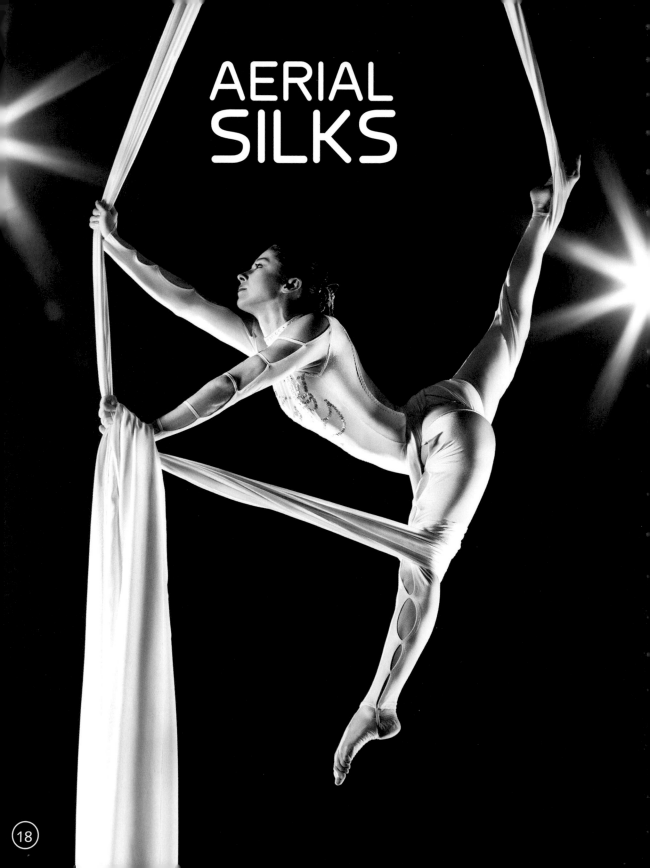

AERIAL SILKS

What's up next, you wonder. An acrobat walks into the ring. A silk loop hangs from the ceiling. It looks like a ribbon. Like a human spider, the acrobat climbs up and spins around the loop of shiny fabric. These loops of fabric are called aerial silks. The performer climbs, twirls, and twists on what seems like the thinnest of supports. She wraps herself up, and then drops, catching herself in the silks without falling.

What's the trick behind these aerial silks? Even though they look shiny and slippery, these loops are not actually made of real silk, but a stronger fabric. Still, the material is slippery. It does not provide much friction against the performer's body. Friction is the force that keeps an object from moving freely against another surface. Because performers have less friction helping hold them up, body strength is very important. Great body strength helps them grip the fabric more tightly and fight against slipping.

DON'T TRY THIS AT HOME

TRY THIS INSTEAD

Experiment with friction using a playground slide and different objects. Collect several items such as a toy car, a book, a shoe with a rubber sole, and a wooden block. Test them to see how quickly each moves down the slide. Set them at the top, but don't push them. Let them slide on their own. Which object went the farthest? Which slid down the fastest? Is there a difference between a metal slide and a plastic slide?

CIRCUS FACT
On June 24, 2015, 30 acrobats set a world record by performing on aerial silks all at the same time.

CORDE LISSE

A soft cotton rope hangs from the ceiling. A circus performer climbs up to the top. Using his body strength, he swings, flips, and then hangs by one leg. He spins around the rope. It looks as if he is dancing with it. The intensity takes your breath away!

What is this rope and how does the performer manage do these tricks around it? This act is corde lisse, which means "smooth rope." Friction again is at work. That's the force that keeps the performer from slipping off the rope. Corde lisse performers must also acquire great arm and upper body strength. That's how they hold themselves at an angle to the rope.

CIRCUS FACT

Spanish web is an act similar to corde lisse. At the top of the rope is a loop. Performers hang from the loop with their hands or feet. A person called the web setter stands on the ground and spins the rope. The rope keeps spinning while the performer is on it. The spinning motion allows the performer's body to move out and away from the rope.

PERCH POLE

These high-flying circus acts aren't over yet! Two performers enter the center stage. One holds a tall pole. The second performer, a flier, climbs to the top. The first performer steadies the pole. He raises it onto his shoulders. Then onto his head! Then he lowers it to a special belt with a holder. The flier performs on the top of the perch pole, balancing, spinning, and doing a headstand! His final feat? Holding himself out at a 90-degree angle like a flag.

What's the most important science element at work here? Balance. The holder must balance the pole and move himself as the weight above shifts. Whenever the flier changes position, the holder adjusts himself to keep the pole upright. He must keep the flier's center of mass directly above him. Otherwise, the pole will tip, and the flier will fall. The holder and the flier must be tuned in to each other's movements perfectly. They practice for weeks on end. Each member must know how any change in his position will affect his partner.

DON'T
TRY THIS AT HOME

TRY THIS INSTEAD

Experiment with center of mass by balancing objects in the palm of your hand. Start with a ruler. What do you have to do with your hand to balance the ruler? Try other objects, such as a pencil with an eraser or a yardstick. Are longer objects easier or more difficult to balance?

CIRCUS FACT

During the Great Depression in the 1930s, there was a fad called flagpole sitting. People climbed to the top of flagpoles and tried to remain there as long as they could.

SPRINGBOARDS

Can this next act beat the last? You better believe it! You look out at the stage. It's empty except for a sloping wooden board. Suddenly, music begins to play. Several performers run out. They jump onto the board, one after another. The board launches them into the air. They twist and flip as they fly. They land on the shoulders of other performers who stand nearby. The crowd gasps in astonishment.

How does the springboard help performers leap so high? The science behind a springboard is hidden in its springs. One or two springs rest underneath the board. When the performer runs and jumps onto the springboard, the springs compress. Compressed, the springs are holding **elastic potential energy**. This is the energy that is stored in the springs that came from the performer's initial jump. As the performer jumps off, that stored energy is converted into the **kinetic energy** of the performer, launching him up into the air. Kinetic energy is energy of motion.

elastic potential energy–the stored energy within an object produced when stretching or squeezing it
kinetic energy–the energy of motion

DON'T
TRY THIS AT HOME

TRY THIS INSTEAD

To see elastic potential energy and kinetic energy at work, try this experiment. All you need is a retractable ballpoint pen and a table or desk. Hold the pen upside down. Press it down onto the table or desk so that the clicker is compressed against the surface. Quickly let go. Does the pen jump? Inside the pen is a spring that compresses as you hold it down just like the springs in a springboard.

TRAMPOLINES

It's the final act. Don't fret! This last performance is sure to amaze. A performer scrambles onto a trampoline. Two others hold a long jump rope between them. Soon the first performer is skipping rope as he jumps high into the air. He begins to add twists and flips. The trampoline shoots him higher and higher. It's amazing!

How does the trampoline give the performer so much height? Trampolines provide a great example of physics at work. Jumping up and down on a trampoline shows the **conservation of energy** quite well. Conservation of energy means that the total energy of a system, such as the trampoline plus the jumper, remains constant and only changes forms. During the bounce, the energy changes forms. It begins as elastic potential energy stored briefly in the trampoline. It changes to kinetic energy of the person flying into the air. Then it changes again to **gravitational potential energy** as the person peaks high above the trampoline.

CIRCUS FACT

On April 8, 2014, Eric, Sean, and T.J. Kennedy set a Guinness World Record for the highest team trampoline bounce. With Eric and T.J. also jumping to make him bounce higher, Sean Kennedy bounced 22 feet, 1 inch (6.7 meters) into the air.

conservation of energy—a principle stating that the total energy of an isolated system remains constant
gravitational potential energy—the energy of an object that arises in relation to another object with mass, and which depends on the distance between the two objects

CIRCUS SAFETY

High-flying circus acts can amaze and stun an audience. But when not done appropriately, they can badly hurt or even kill performers. Aerial performers use safety techniques and equipment to make sure that they can entertain people while also putting themselves in the least amount of danger possible.

All high-flying circus equipment is rigged a certain way. Rigging is a set of safety lines and harnesses. Performers wear them so that even if they fall off a trapeze or a platform, they won't hit the ground.

High-flying performers often use safety nets too. These are large nets set up underneath the act and stretched tightly. Stretching the net keeps it from sagging when the flier hits it. If a flier falls, the net catches him. Sometimes thick pads are below. Performers learn how to land safely during a fall to spread the impact and avoid injury.

Performers follow special safety procedures. They learn to time their acts perfectly. Catchers stay close in case they need to catch another performer. Safety procedures and equipment don't guarantee that performers will never get hurt. But they help keep circus acts safe and entertaining.

angular momentum (ANG-gyu-lur moh-MEN-tuhm)—a measure of an object's rotation, involving mass, shape, and speed

axis (AK-siss)—the straight line around which an object rotates

center of mass (SEN-tur UVH MASS)—the point in an object around which its mass is evenly distributed

conservation of energy (kon-sur-VAY-shuhn UHV EN-ur-jee)—a principle stating that the total energy of an isolated system remains constant

elastic potential energy (ee-LAS-tik puh-TEN-shuhl EN-ur-jee)—the stored energy within an object produced when stretching or squeezing it

friction (FRIK-shuhn)—a force that opposes the relative motion of two or more surfaces in contact

force (FORS)—an interaction, such as a push or pull, that changes the motion of an object

gravity (GRAV-uh-tee)—an attractive force that exists between any two objects, including between Earth and everything on it

gravitational potential energy (GRAV-uh-shun-uhl puh-TEN-shuhl EN-ur-jee)— the energy of an object that arises in relation to another object with mass, and which depends on the distance between the two objects

kinetic energy (ki-NET-ik EN-ur-jee)—the energy of motion

pendulum (PEN-dju-lem)—a body hung from a fixed point that swings freely back and forth

rotate (ROH-tate)—to turn in a circle

static (STAH-tik)—having the quality of being at rest

static equilibrium (STAH-tik e-kwa-LIB-ree-em)—a state of balance between two or more opposing forces

torque (TORK)—the tendency of a force to rotate an object about an axis

READ MORE

Doudna, Kelly. *The Kid's Book of Simple, Everyday Science*. Minneapolis, Minn.: Scarletta Kids, 2013.

Gogerly, Liz. *Circuses*. Explore! London: Wayland, 2017.

Mercer, Bobby. *Junk Drawer Physics: 50 Awesome Experiments that Don't Cost a Thing*. Junk Drawer Science. Chicago: Chicago Review Press, 2014.

Royston, Angela. *Forces and Motion*. Essential Physical Science. Chicago: Heinemann Library, 2014.

Turnbull, Stephanie. *Circus Skills*. Super Skills. Mankato, Minn.: Smart Apple Media, 2013.

INTERNET SITES

Use FactHound to find Internet sites related to this book.

Visit *www.facthound.com*

Just type in 9781515772842 and go.

INDEX